First Daughters: Empowering the Kingdom

A DEVOTIONAL FOR WOMEN CALLED TO RECLAIM THEIR CROWN

MIRLINE AUGUSTIN

Contents

Introduction

HER CALL TO THE THRONE

D aughters are nurturers of their family. They hold the strings and bonds of their home's heart.

They are entitled to the inheritance and blessings of the Father through relationship with the Son, Jesus. They are the ones who carry the spiritual attributes and character of our Heavenly Father: **unconditional love, inner peace, harmony, justice, optimism, humility,** and **responsibility.**

Daughters continue to reach the lives of many across nations. They address numerous situations with wisdom and discover solutions for disparities while promoting human kindness.

Yet, in the life of a daughter, she will endure many false teachings: teachings shaped by the wounds of her heart and the misguided stories of those around her. Because of her vulnerability to receiving and giving love, she is often trapped in idolatry, rejection, and abuse. She is stuck in spiritual and emotional bondage, even though she was not formed for the pleasures of this world, but for **sanctification** and **deliverance** from its evil.

Look at what the Apostle Paul shares in Romans 8:

> [15] For you did not receive the spirit of slavery to fall back into fear. Instead, you received the Spirit of adoption, by whom we cry out, 'Abba, Father!'
>
> Romans 8:15 CSB

Spirits of fear, rejection, false fate, reliant slavery, and failure are not your inheritance! **You were always His.** You may have been lost in the translations and traumas of the world, but you have always belonged to Him. **You are a daughter, ever returning to your Father.**

As children enduring emotional, physical, or mental pain, we cry out to our Father in our hearts and aloud:

"Abba!" To a daughter, her first love, her Abba, is om-nipresent, all-knowing, and full of potent mercy. He is the supreme love that overshadows every flaw, every blemish, and every discord in our lives. He sees. He knows. He shelters.

With His outstretched arm, He calls us home:

> [6]I will say to the north, 'Give them up!' and to the south, 'Do not hold them back!' Bring my sons from far away, and my daughters from the ends of the earth—[7] everyone who bears my name and is created for my glory. I have formed them; indeed, I have made them."
>
> Isaiah 43:6-7 CSB

You were not made in the image of this world, but in the image of our Lord Jesus Christ. Your Father created you in His likeness, presenting you to this world through two people, your natural father and mother.

Evil cannot create life; it can only prey on the living. Out of this darkness, immorality and wickedness are formed. Yet there is no love like a father's love. Those who have received a false love at the hands of the enemy: love that calls upon death and feeds on the bosom of destruction and deceit, will face the judgment of our Almighty Lord, Jesus Christ. So be it.

The world keeps filling the minds of God's children with confusion. It teaches them to wear the image of their idols. They are dressed in garments of self-hate and duplicity, believing these are acceptable in the eyes of their false gods. However, the Lord has spoken. He is calling the nations, even those that despise His words, using them as a mirror to reveal the evil and treachery of their hearts.

Even now, the Almighty continues to grant **mercy** and **compassion** to those who genuinely seek Him: His light, path, and direction. In the fields of rejection, slavery, and confusion, He still calls His daughters. He still prepares a place for them at His table, the table of Heaven. **Daughter, you are called to the throne.** And you shall forever remain there, praising with good news and joy to the lost children of the world. You are called to speak to those trapped in fear and ignorance, those preyed upon by the predators of this world, and those whose crowns still wait to be worn.

Your Father sees you. Your Father is calling you. Your Father will place His crown upon your head.

> [16] The Spirit himself testifies together with our spirit that we are God's children, [17] and if children, also heirs—heirs of God and coheirs with Christ—if indeed we suffer with him so that we may also be glorified with him.
>
> Romans 8:16-17 CSB

Daughter, you are His.
You are called.
You are crowned.
You are home.

Chapter 1

Eve

His First Daughter

Eve receives the backlash for all the pain and suffering that women endure on this side of eternity. She is blamed, hated, and charged with bringing death to all that was once good. Despite people's opinions of her, her Father still loved her. He was disappointed, yes, but not distant. He continued to demonstrate His love through guidance and care.

She still had a purpose. She had been assigned to continue life on earth: to multiply, nurture, and help. Eve did not know the full story, nor did she need to. She only knew her assignment: **to help.**

God created Adam and placed him above the animals and all of creation. He authorized him as ruler over the sea, the land, and every living thing that breathed. Yet in the beauty of His creation, God noticed something: all creatures had a companion, but Adam was alone.

And so, in divine wisdom and timing, God caused a deep sleep to come over Adam: a holy rest, a coma of trust. Adam had no awareness of the Lord's plan, but in obedience, he surrendered to it. God did not ask for Adam's assistance. He did not need his opinion or request for what came next. He had a plan, and in that plan, He created Eve.

> [21] So the Lord God caused a deep sleep to come over the man, and he slept. God took one of his ribs and closed the flesh at that place. [22] Then the Lord God made the rib he had taken from the man into a woman and brought her to the man.
>
> Genesis 2:21-22 CSB

Eve was created specifically for Adam, not by his request, but by God's divine design. He could have chosen a Naomi, a Mary, or a Ruth. However, it was not their season. It was Eve's.

God created her in His own image: a reflection of righteousness, honor, servitude, humility, and, most importantly, obedience. God knew the importance of selecting a wife who would understand her role, not just in Adam's life, but in carrying out the will of God's Kingdom. Out of all the extraordinary daughters in His eternal pocket, Eve was chosen. She was the one who fit the assignment for that moment in history.

As first daughters, we carry a heavy mantle: full of responsibilities as mothers, wives, daughters, and leaders. The first daughter often carries the weight of the family's name, reputation, and spiritual identity. We are born into expectations we did not create. We walk into roles we did not fully choose.

Eve was the first in line without a detailed plan. She was given breath and placed under the leadership of her father and husband, entrusted to their words to provide, protect, and secure her existence and future.

The enemy, of course, targets that. It points out our flaws, ridicules our obedience, and amplifies every insecurity. It mocks what we do not yet understand and preys on our vulnerability. It uses distraction, deception, and false worship to lure us away from our crown.

But our Father still shepherds us. He still provides. He still protects. He offers wisdom to those who ask and identity to those who return.

Salvation is free. But it must be received, not by force, but by choice. Free will is a gift. Salvation is the result of surrendering to God's will and accepting Jesus Christ as Lord and Savior. I am here to remind you that you were created with purpose, daughter. And like Eve, you may not have all the details. But you were chosen for this season, this assignment, and this moment in His Kingdom.

Prayer

Father,

I come before You and pray over my sister who has been thrown into deserts without water: harboring disbelief as she stands in positions and roles she has yet to fulfill. Lord, I ask that You reinstate her confidence in You. Remind her that Your plans far exceed her limited agenda, and silence the voice of the enemy who would persuade her that she is defeated. Father, I pray that You keep her grounded close to Your roots. Pour into her Your wisdom and essence, so that she will continue to carry the mantle You have bestowed upon her. May she always know that she is, and forever will be, Your daughter.

In Jesus' Name,

Amen

Scan the QR code below for the reflection video related to this chapter.

Chapter 1

CHAPTER 2

The Daughter with the Issue

When we think about our past, present, and the possibilities of our future, we often desire greatness. We desire fulfillment in our finances, relationships, and families. We seek out knowledge through community engagement and education.

As daughters, we convince ourselves that all of this can be earned through strenuous effort: pouring ourselves into academia, careers, motherhood, and ministry. We strive for a sense of security.

We hold tightly to independence. We pride ourselves on being able to do for ourselves, without asking for help or leaning on anyone. However, without purpose, who are we and to whom are we called?

As daughters, we are taught to love, nurture, comfort, and uplift others: physically, spiritually, emotionally. We are raised to believe that a daughter is the heart of her father, the very reason he rises to protect, honor, and stand tall. However, many daughters today live without the presence of a father.

When life gets hard and issues arise, who do we call on? For many of us, it is a father figure we wish we had; a man to show up with wisdom, provision, and strength. For some, it is a brother, an uncle, or a grandfather. Despite these males who step in, at the core, there is the same need: **to feel protected**. We want to know someone is near with a firm but gentle hand.

Throughout history, daughters have been pushed aside. We were not given the same space as men. We were assigned roles as midwives and wet nurses. We could not be seen in public without a male escort. We could not even access education, and yet, we endured. Even in limited spaces, we found purpose.

However, what happened to daughters who did not meet the criteria for usefulness? Where are the barren, the broken, and the outcast?

In Matthew 9:20, we meet a daughter like that: the woman with an issue of blood. She had been bleeding for twelve excruciating years. As daughters, we know the journey of womanhood begins with our bodies changing, often painfully. A typical cycle may last 28 days, sometimes ranging between 21 to 35 days. However, this woman's cycle never ended. For twelve years, her body was in turmoil. Her emotions were triggered. Her pain was constant. Her future was unclear.

She could not marry. She could not work as a wet nurse or midwife. She could not be favored socially. She was shut out of opportunities, relationships, and even society. She became invisible. She was isolated, unmarried, without prospects, and suffering from shame.

Even though humiliation, depression, and hopelessness kept her company, she still had faith. She believed that just one touch of Jesus' garment could change everything. She saw her only chance for healing, not in people's approval, but in the presence of the Savior. She lowered herself in a room full of people. She risked being seen in her issue, and she reached. She touched. She believed. Then, she was made whole.

Daughter, what is your issue? Is it family? Finances? Illness? Shame? Sin? Do not let your issue become your identity. Do not let what is hurting you keep you hidden. You are still seen, loved, and called.

God is not afraid of your issue, and He is not withholding your healing. You have the Holy Spirit within you. You are the one He has been waiting to restore. Yes, daughter, the seas will part. However, your faith must step first. Work your ministry. Show up for your calling. Let God have the final word.

Prayer

Father,

Hear my request to honor You in all our ways; whether physical, emotional, or mental. We want to glorify You and Your heavenly Kingdom despite our circumstances. Father, my sister is grieving in ways that only You truly understand. You have seen her pain. You have witnessed her affliction firsthand. Reveal Your truth within her heart, Lord. Surround her with caring spaces and loving voices that uplift, rejoice, and reflect kindness and compassion. Remind her that she is still Your daughter, even in her pain. Let her feel Your presence so she knows she is **not alone**. You are her **Jehovah Rapha**, the Lord who heals, and by faith, she shall be healed. For Your Word declares: "I am the Lord who heals you." in *Exodus 15:26* and "Your faith has made you whole." in *Luke 17:19*. May she rest in the promises of Your Word and continue to praise You through it all.

In Jesus' Name,

Amen

Scan the QR code below for the reflection video related to this chapter.

Chapter 2

CHAPTER 3

Her Distraction to Discernment

D aily living is a blessing here on Earth. We continue to find ways to empower our lives through our work and deeds: by helping one another, our communities, children, and kinfolk.

As daughters, we rely on the wisdom and teachings of our mothers, grandmothers, aunts, sisters, teachers, and elders to shape our understanding of identity and purpose in society.

Daughters are deeply impressionable because we often rely heavily on intellect. We think our way through life, but we also attach our hearts to the very things that have historically been used against us.

Our understanding is intentional and rooted in hope. We long to satisfy not just our own desire for a better future, but also that of others. We are hope-carriers. However, that same hope can become clouded by greed, envy, uncertainty, distrust, anger, and even idolatry.

In Genesis 3, our fall from communion with Heaven was initiated by the enemy, not because we were weak, but because we held **potential**. The enemy saw something divine and powerful in us, so he devised a plan.

But the Lord, in His mercy, shared the consequence; He allowed it, yes, but it was never without covering. The enemy's exit from Heaven came not because he lost power, but because of his rebellion. It was our **potential** that made him cunning in his approach.

Scripture says:

> [1]Now the serpent was the most cunning of all the wild animals the Lord God had made." He said to the woman, "Did God really say you can't eat from any tree in the garden?" [2] The woman said to the serpent, "We may eat the fruit from the trees in the garden. [3] But about the fruit of the tree in the

middle of the garden, God said, 'You must not eat it or touch it, or you will die.'"

Genesis 3:1-3 CSB

And the serpent whispered:

4 "No! You will certainly not die," the serpent said to the woman. **5** "In fact, God knows that when you eat it your eyes will be opened and you will be like God, knowing good and evil."

Genesis 3:4-5 CSB

The woman saw that the tree was good for food, beautiful to look at, and desirable for gaining wisdom. She ate. She gave it to Adam. He ate. Then, their eyes were opened. When I read this passage, I realized: Eve believed what she ate was good for her and convinced her husband of the same. Because they trusted each other deeply, they followed the deception together.

What about the serpent? He was already in the garden. That struck me. The enemy was there, in a holy place, camouflaged in beauty, cunning, and full of wisdom. He was once a **cherub** and adorned in jewels. That means he had glory, position, and spiritual access... and still chose deceit (Ezekiel 28).

So, he transformed. He did not become something harmless like a bird or a rabbit, but a serpent: a symbol of fear, deception, and silence. Then he whispered, "Do not listen to God. He just does not want you to be like Him." It is the same lie today.

The enemy still uses that tactic: He watches your potential. He sees the favor in your life. Then, he tries to blend in, camouflaging himself through people, opportunities, or situations that look good but do not align with God.

Have you ever encountered someone who sees your potential and tries to edge in, not to build with you, but to distract you? That is exactly what the **serpent** did. He did not show up angry or obvious. He showed up "familiar." He used proximity to disarm Eve's discernment.

The enemy fears **the divine delicacy** with which God created you. Eve was not created overnight. She was formed in the image of God, in deep spiritual intimacy; a relationship between a Father and His first daughter. She knew: "That's my dad. He'll protect me. He'll never leave me." She was not going to go against His command, but confusion entered when she encountered a voice that sounded like it had authority. "He was here before me. He must know what God meant. I misunderstood."

That is how the enemy works; he uses false wisdom to introduce doubt. However, the enemy does not have the full picture. He sees your potential, but not God's plans. God will **never** reveal His blueprints to the enemy.

So, what does the enemy do? He twists the truth. He sows questions. He says, "You did not hear God clearly. You misunderstood. God is holding something back." It is a distraction dressed up as discernment.

Despite the enemy's lies, **God is still good. He is still just. He is still merciful.**

Even when we fall for the lie, He makes a way of restoration. Today I am thankful that we live on this side of eternity: after Christ, where grace and truth go hand-in-hand.

God still has a plan. His will shall still be accomplished. When we trust Him with faith, even when we do not understand it all, He aligns, covers, and saves us. No one is taking your seat, daughter. We have wisdom now. From this day forward, we confirm everything with **our Heavenly Father**.

I appreciate the intentions of others who try to offer insight. But I have learned: "Thank you; I'll take that to the Lord in prayer." Go with God.

Prayer

Father,

I come before You to place a covering, like that of Moses, as he walked through parted seas during testaments of spiritual slavery and influence. I pray that this daughter, who faces spirits of division and confusion, will stand firm in the truth. Let her recognize that the **Lord of Armies** is on her side, and she will crossover into **Victory** in peace. May Your love continue to resurrect over her life. Keep her steadfast in prayer, even while under pressure, and cloaked in the covering of the **blood of Christ**. Let her rise and glorify Your name through her works and deeds in the Kingdom. May her life encourage those still searching for You to run straight into Your love and wisdom, and into the embrace of You.

In Jesus' Name,

Amen

Scan the QR code below for the reflection video related to this chapter.

Chapter 3

CHAPTER 4

His Secret Bloom

Quiet. **Awkward. Misfit. Belittled. Different. Ignored. Weird.** With unmatched beauty, she remains unavailable to the world. Often left out and undisturbed, she has grown accustomed to not partaking in the spoils of a fallen world. Placed on a high shelf, away from the peering eyes of others; She may seem forgotten. However, she has not forgotten.

Her standards are set by her Heavenly Father and often intimidate those not aligned with the Kingdom of God. This daughter has endured pain and trials from a young age and continues to navigate life with wisdom and favor. The Holy Spirit accompanies her daily as she prays, studies, and worships. She has been given rare gifts and often wonders why she thinks, feels, and moves so differently. As she grows closer to the Lord, she is tested and challenged in her relationships. Many times, she has cried out for peace and stability within her own mind, body, and soul.

The enemy has desired her since birth. He places boulders and mountains in her path, hoping to cause her to stumble into fear, panic, heartbreak, abuse, addiction, and exhaustion. She has been chosen from the beginning. Her story is unique, and she continues to draw near to her Heavenly Father in ways the world cannot comprehend. He instills in her wisdom, grace, patience, and obedience through Scripture and intimacy. As she abides in Him, she is reminded each day that **her story is still unfolding in the Lord's hands**. She is no longer misguided or misunderstood. She is ministering through her worship and vulnerability. The Lord has a perfect timing for her unveiling. He alone will reveal her with the glory that matches her purpose.

As with **Queen Esther,** an orphan raised by her cousin Mordecai, after the death of her parents, she was kept hidden and filled with wisdom and the knowledge of God. Though a Jewish exile under Persian rule, God preserved her as His secret bloom. He revealed her at the right time to become a beacon of light and voice of deliverance. When the moment came, Esther became queen and used her favor and position to persuade King Ahasuerus to revoke the decree of extermination against the Jews. Her obedience to Mordecai rewrote the future of a nation. Look at what Mordecai told Esther:

> **14** ...Who knows, perhaps you have come to your royal position for such a time as this.
>
> Esther 4:14 CSB

The King, enamored by her grace and beauty, granted her request and protected her people.

Daughter, God has chosen **you** to be a voice, a light, and a guide for those who have been silenced, afraid, and marginalized. Your obedience can impact generations. Though your time may feel delayed, God's timing is perfect. Your "yes" today could be the world's "thank you" tomorrow. Let Him continue to bloom you in secret until the Kingdom beholds what He has planted in you.

Prayer

Father,

I come before You and ask that You shield this daughter who has felt alone, misunderstood, and unaware of the power she carries. Your Word declares in Psalm 46:5, "God is within her, she will not fall." I pray she finds her worth in You and not in the voices of the world, which lead only to instability. Let her know she has been chosen for this purpose and that her royal positioning is tied to the calling You've placed within her. We give You praise and honor as You reign forever in our hearts. Thank You for Your mercy, grace, and unconditional love. Thank You for who You continue to be in our lives.

In Jesus' Name,

Amen

Scan the QR code below for the reflection video related to this chapter.

Chapter 4

CHAPTER 5

The Silenced Daughter

"You are not a victim. You are a **victor**. You walk in the glory of God."

P urity is the essence of righteousness, just as turmoil is the result of sin and disobedience. Regret is a path we often walk when facing tragic loss. However, through prayer and forgiveness, we learn to find vindication. When injustice strikes, our first instinct may be retaliation: to make the offender feel the weight of their actions. On the other hand, in God's Kingdom, justice comes through truth, healing, and redemption.

Today, young women suffer staggering losses of innocence and safety which leads to emotional confusion and lasting trauma. Many of these wounds were inflicted in environments lacking stability and godly protection. Some were exposed to inappropriate behavior at a young age: often by trusted family members, close friends, or respected leaders. The pressure to behave or appear a certain way: to make others feel comfortable with their beauty or presence, leaves many daughters vulnerable and unguarded.

In the story of **Dinah** (found in Genesis 35), the daughter of Leah and Jacob, we witness the pain of a silenced daughter. While visiting the city of Shechem to meet local women, Dinah was seen by the son of Hamor the Hivite, the region's chief. Captivated by her beauty, he made a tragic choice: he took what was not his. Dinah, simply walking in her own right, was violated. She had no intention of being seen or harmed. Likely imagining a peaceful day of laughter and fellowship, she instead encountered a tragedy that shattered her ability to trust, feel safe, and rest within her own body and mind. Not only was she violated, she was met with **silence**. Her father Jacob grieved but remained quiet. When Hamor approached to request Dinah's hand in marriage, claiming it was out of affection, her brothers responded with vengeance and killed every man in the city.

How many daughters today have suffered at the hands of someone they trusted: a friend, family member, or person of influence? How many live in silence, still burdened by shame and fear, while the world moves on without noticing? The weight of it breeds guilt, anxiety, and isolation. The injustice speaks loudly, yet the girl's voice is silenced.

Daughter, this **will not** be your story. God has not forgotten you. He hears your cries of shame and grief. He sees every memory that replays in your mind. He is your **defender, comforter,** and **redeemer.** He has never left your side. Jesus died for your healing and rose to declare that **death and shame will not have the final word over your life.** He is the ultimate vengeance for your honor. His blood speaks on your behalf.

We now speak life to your broken heart. We cover the endless nights of torment with the light of truth. We reclaim the power that was stolen from you. You are greater than anything that ever tried to belittle you. The army of God surrounds you. The lies of the enemy have no authority. You are not a victim. **You are a victor. You walk in the glory of God.** You are the daughter of the King.

***

My sister, forgive yourself. Forgive those who hurt you—not for their sake, but for your freedom.

Prayer

Father,

I lift up every daughter who has been silenced, shamed, humiliated, and burdened with trauma that has plagued her life. I ask You to remove every lingering residue of guilt, sorrow, and torment that continues to manifest through triggered memories and painful encounters. Let her past be sealed as a forgotten chapter, so she may step into the new story You have already written for her. May she rise with confidence and a renewed mind. Let her be fully restored by the seeds of healing You've planted within her soul. Father, I pray my sister will reclaim the crown that was stolen by the enemy's lie that her worth could be taken. We bind that lie now! Remind her that she belongs to You. Remind her she is covered in Your peace, wrapped in Your love, and strengthened by Your Spirit. She is not forgotten. She is not forsaken. She is the daughter of a King.

In Jesus' Name,

Amen

Because this chapter deals with deep trauma, no video reflection is provided to avoid re-triggering sensitive experiences. We invite you instead to visit **gemsrooted.org** for additional resources, prayers, and supportive guidance designed to help you process safely and in God's timing. Remember, you are not alone. Healing is a journey, and the Father's love restores even the most silenced voices.

Chapter 5 (Resources)

CHAPTER 6

Her Spiritual Womb

What seeds are you planting in others? For we are grounded and rooted in the source, which is Christ. As we sprout into a beautiful tree, we are called to produce fruits of the Spirit in a world filled with hunger, injustice, pride, attention-seeking, and false sacrifices. What fruits are we bearing to nourish those desperately seeking shelter in a realm compromised in flesh, spirit, and mind? How are we reaching the undelivered?

Consider those who are still trapped in the womb of a broken heart: forgotten, unforgiven, unloved, and abused. Many continue to feed on false doctrines of idolatry, mental illness, and lost identity. Our ability to feed the spiritually hungry is deeply connected to our obedience to God. Disobedience comes at a cost; it can even manifest as physical affliction when we suppress the Word of God. On the contrary, in divine timing, obedience becomes a blessing, not only for us, but for the unborn souls of this world who are waiting to experience true love and healing from the Father.

In Luke 1, Elizabeth was considered righteous before the Lord, yet she remained childless and had grown old. Her husband Zechariah, a priest, was visited by the angel Gabriel while serving in the temple. Because of Zechariah's fervent prayers and obedience, God declared that his wife would bear a son. However, Zechariah doubted the power of God due to his wife's age. Consequently, he was made mute until the child's birth.

When we doubt God's power and the wisdom of His Word, we erase the very existence of life and truth. Our words are powerful! With just a single utterance from God, we came into being. So, to silence the voice of doubt, God silenced Zechariah. His testimony reminds us that our obedience connects others to the Word and to the very existence of Jesus Christ. Even without speaking, our lives can testify and give God all the glory.

Mary, too, was visited by the angel Gabriel in Luke 1. She was considered holy and pure in God's eyes. Gabriel told her she would bear the Son of God. Mary questioned, but not in doubt. Her question was rooted in wonder at how God, who does not follow man's logic, would accomplish this. She said, "I have not known a man". Gabriel revealed that the Holy Spirit would come upon her, and the power of the Most High would overshadow her. The child would be called the Son of God. Gabriel encouraged her by pointing to Elizabeth, her relative, who was also miraculously pregnant in her old age. He emphasized:

37 "For nothing will be impossible with God".

Luke 1:37 CSB

The assignments God ordains for our lives are always greater than we can imagine. Imagine if Elizabeth had rejected her calling out of disbelief; she would not have been the example Mary needed to believe that all things are possible.

Our testimonies, trials, and triumphs provide hope for others. When we share our struggles, we share stories that anchor others to the Word of God. When Elizabeth and Mary finally met, Elizabeth's baby leapt in her womb at the presence of Jesus. Even in the womb, the Holy Spirit was at work. Christ's presence stirred life. Elizabeth later gave birth to John the Baptist, the one who would prepare the way for the Lord. Elizabeth's relationship with God, her obedience, and her womb birthed the one who baptized the Messiah. Our divine purpose connects us to the will of the Father and brings salvation to the undelivered. We carry seeds of wisdom, love, compassion, and spiritual fruit that are meant to be sown into others.

To the daughters who feel barren in their spiritual walk, reconnect with women who have walked these paths. Uplift the younger ones and draw near to the Lord. Do not tear down the altar He has built in you just because it stands in solitude. The Holy Spirit still dwells there. The altar in you belongs to the Lord. God your Father will exalt you in ways the world cannot. Your time is not over. He will carry you through and clothe you with a garment of glory that can be seen from miles away. He will be proud to boast about His favored daughter.

Prayer: For Her Spiritual Womb

Father,

I come before You on behalf of one of Your daughters who is struggling to understand her purpose during this season of barrenness. She may not yet see her worth, but she longs to surrender her womb, her place of purpose, back to You. Only You can mend what man cannot. Let her feel Your presence as You restore the broken pieces and return what was stolen from her. The enemy will do all he can to persuade her that the battle is lost, but we know, Lord, that **Your Word is final and the battle belongs to You**. Draw her into Your rest. Let her lay down the weapons of the world and take up the **weapons of Your Word.** Holy Spirit, cradle her in peace as she sleeps. Sing over her, Lord. Wrap her in the powerful and comforting arms of the Father. **Let Your will be done.**

In Jesus' Name,

Amen

Scan the QR code below for the reflection video related to this chapter.

Chapter 6

CHAPTER 7

Her Covenant

What covenants are we keeping on this side of eternity that interfere with our relationship with God and place our purpose in limbo? By covenants, I'm referring to worldly promises and altars that we have given life to and continue to feed. I often think about the initial promises made to God through Abraham, Isaac, and Jacob, and how they were kept and strengthened through generations. God our Father is a promise-keeping Father who adores His children with blessings, gifts, and grace. He loves us immensely and never fails to show His love through daily teachings, protection, provision, and comfort.

The world has worked its way into our minds. It has deepened wounds of insecurity, inadequacy, and self-driven guilt. It continues to drive a wedge between our God-given purpose and our ability to serve the Kingdom. Our immediate needs do not compare to the needs of the Kingdom. This guarantees a battle of the mind. As daughters, we search for understanding and acceptance in the world, but we fail to realize that our future is not in our bloodstained hands; it is in the hands of the righteous Lord.

We are called to defeat the enemy and his schemes to commit to self-denial. However, we rely on self-preservation. We harvest the enemy's fruit of deception and surrender our Kingdom rights in the process. Our covenant was never created for the enemy's growing kingdom. It was created to defeat the agenda of the world. We must speak the name of Jesus into every walking corpse still eating, sleeping, and multiplying death with every encounter.

24 Then Jesus said to his disciples, "If anyone wants to follow after me, let him deny himself, take up his cross, and follow me.

Matthew 16:24 CSB

What parts of the cross have become so heavy that we feel the need to lay it down from time to time? Some of us drop it on Wednesdays, hang it on the doorframe, and forget about it until the next Bible study. The world is going in the wrong direction. To follow the world is to walk the path of destruction. Many have chased its trends, fashion, lifestyles, and statuses, seeking more for ourselves while slowly drifting from salvation. As daughters, we continue to compete with the world, failing to recognize that it's hindering our spiritual growth. When we walk daily with the Lord: speaking, writing, singing, teaching, bearing fruit, and using the gifts He has given us, the world becomes irrelevant. To follow Christ is to fix our eyes on the eternal future with God our Savior and never look back to the brokenness of the world.

In Genesis 13, we meet Lot, Abraham's nephew. He was taken into the city of Sodom and Gomorrah with his wife and two daughters. Because the outcry of sin had reached the Lord, He planned to destroy the city in Genesis 19. Three angels were first sent to Abraham's tent and informed him of God's plan. Later, two of those angels approached the gateway of Sodom, where they were met by Lot, unaware of their divine identity. He persuaded them to stay the night and prepared a meal. That night, the men of the city demanded Lot release the strangers so they could defile them. Lot pleaded with them to stop and even offered his two virgin daughters in desperation. Ignorantly, the men, blinded by their lust, rejected the offer and threatened to harm Lot himself. The angels then struck the men with blindness and warned Lot to flee with his family. Though Lot hesitated, the Lord's compassion moved the angels to seize the hands of Lot, his wife, and his daughters, leading them safely out of the city.

When God has a plan for you: when your assignment is written and sealed, nothing and no one can prevent it from being fulfilled. Yes, God gives us free will, but for a chosen few, the task is non-negotiable. Remember Jonah? He resisted and ran, but the assignment still came to pass. Likewise, because of the covenant God made with Abraham, Lot was shown favor. His obedience and faith allowed him to witness the presence and power of God firsthand.

Prayer

Father,

Help Your daughter to uncover the covenants she has made with herself that do not glorify Your name or advance Your Kingdom. Grant her the wisdom to break free and remove any stain of the world that continues to dilute her destiny. Give her discernment and strength, that she may find protection from deception and impurity. Release and remove every old covenant that has distorted the vision You have for her. Restore the crown that has long sat on the shelf. Forgive her, Lord, for she lacked knowledge and nearly perished. Yet I thank You for giving her another chance to receive Your glory in Your loving hands. Lord, let every altar built for man be destroyed, as Your daughters rise to rebuild, restore, and renew the altars for You, just as David did in the book of 1 Chronicles. Let Your daughter sing Your praise forever. Reintroduce Your Spirit to dwell within her, now and forevermore.

In Jesus' Name,
Amen

Scan the QR code below for the reflection video related to this chapter.

Chapter 7

CHAPTER 8

The Spirit of Miriam

False teaching is a rejected doctrine that the Holy Word and Spirit refuse to accept.

In today's society, many individuals present themselves as something they are not. They accuse others of being false witnesses, Christians, and prophets. The enemy thrives on lies and deceit to foster false identities. When we take on these deceptive images, we replace the Christlike identities that God has given us, seeking to please either ourselves or the people around us.

In the books of Exodus and Numbers, Moses walked with his siblings and was chosen among them to be the leader of the Israelites. God specifically preserved Moses during a time of high infant mortality, economic and spiritual adversity, and slavery. His divine plan ensured that Moses' lineage would reap the blessings of His promise. Miriam, Moses' older sister, loved him dearly and was entrusted with ensuring his safe captivity within the royal household. His mother, trusting in God's wisdom, relied on Miriam's obedience and faith to help steer Moses' path. Through her trust in the Lord, his safe arrival into the arms of the royal family was granted by the power of God.

Sometimes, we find ourselves in the enemy's territory: sharing time, breaking bread, or even dwelling in their presence. However, because of our covenant with God and the continued obedience of those before us, we remain covered by His grace and power. The weapons formed against us shall never gain strength nor pierce through the plans that the Lord has for us.

Miriam was a mentor, a worshipper, an influencer, and a constant reminder of what obedience to God resembles. However, at some point, she lost focus, falling into the hands of the enemy through self-indulgence, idolatry, and the pettiness of the world. She allowed her title to supersede the divine instructions and expectations of her calling. Many daughters of Christ have walked a similar path, albeit in different ways. Social media has granted us the power to influence many, persuading people to listen to our words and observe our lives. Yet, too often, we operate under the guise of false teachings, self-validation, and worldly desires. We have allowed society to shape our righteous hearing, favoring what the majority (like social media and public opinion) desires to hear. We crave desirability, approval, and validation from the world; however, who are we if we prefer the words of the unrighteous?

During Moses' leadership of the Israelites, Miriam was granted divine favor because of the covenant. However, jealousy crept into her heart and shifted the trajectory of her life. She grew envious of her brother and allowed the enemy to deceive her into thinking that disobedience was the path to freedom. She pursued her own agenda because she believed it would grant her power. She sought to establish her own following. Her disobedience led her so far astray that it angered God, and she was stricken with a physical illness. This led to isolation and an ultimately death.

The choices we make on this side of eternity always lead to either a good or bad outcome. When faith becomes entangled with greed and self-idolatry, God is no longer at the center of our actions. As daughters of Christ, we must be vigilant when working with those whom God has given access to lead. We must learn to submit and lift up the Lord in everything we do.

> [31] So, whether you eat or drink, or whatever you do, do everything for the glory of God.
>
> 1 Corinthians 10:31 CSB

It is for the glory of God, not for the glory of men or women. They do not deserve the praise.

Prayer

Father,

Lord, I come before You, seeking Your presence. I honor the gifts and time we have shared, even in dry seasons. I continue to pursue Your voice and direction amid the noise of this world. Lord, I pray that Your influence empowers your daughter to joyfully share Your Word and Your love. Teach her to savor Your wisdom above the persuasion of the world, and to remain mindful that her time here is limited. Keep her heart anchored to the task of preparing the world for Your return. Regardless of the fame, accolades, money, or temporary power she may encounter in this season, help her stay focused. Lord, protect her from allowing her limited capabilities to cloud her vision with arrogance. Let her continue to search for more of you. Father, I lift up every daughter who is walking through a season like Miriam's. Remind her that You are the center of it all, and that no temporary platform is worth the price of her eternal salvation.

In Jesus' Name,

Amen

Scan the QR code below for the reflection video related to this chapter.

Chapter 8

CHAPTER 9

The Sower

Our spiritual life is based on the seeds we plant in one another. Those seeds encourage the growth of the spiritual fruits: love, patience, joy, peace, kindness, goodness, faithfulness, gentleness, and self-control. The fruits of the Spirit demonstrate that the Holy Spirit is living within us. It also shows that the Holy Spirit continues to guide, teach, fortify, convict, and comfort our spiritual growth through the gifts provided by our Heavenly Father.

In the book of Matthew, Jesus sits with the crowd near the sea and teaches them through parables. Because there were so many people. He sat in the midst of them on a boat to share His message. Though they heard the Word,

some may not have understood it, so He spoke to them
in parables:

> ³ Then he told them many things in parables,
> saying, "Consider the sower who went out to
> sow. ⁴ As he sowed, some seed fell along the
> path, and the birds came and devoured them.
> ⁵ Other seed fell on rocky ground where it
> didn't have much soil, and it grew up quick-
> ly since the soil wasn't deep. ⁶ But when the
> sun came up, it was scorched, and since it
> had no root, it withered away. ⁷ Other seed
> fell among thorns, and the thorns came up
> and choked it. ⁸ Still other seed fell on good
> ground and produced fruit: some a hundred,
> some sixty, and some thirty times what was
> sown. ⁹ Let anyone who has ears listen."
>
> Matthew 13:3-9 CSB

When we look at our lives and how our journey with
Christ reflects the series of decisions and choices we
make, it provides a clear picture of what our responsibilities in the Kingdom of God require. Obedience is sure to

get God's attention. A faithful servant continues to look to the Lord with questioning eyes and an eager heart, ensuring their righteous path is in the hands of the Lord.

God does not take any moment for granted. He continues to place reminders of His presence and mercy in our daily routines: mothering, nurturing, teaching, providing, and strengthening the bonds within our communities. When Jesus explained the parable's meaning, many could see themselves in His metaphor; how narrow the road to righteousness is compared to the broadness of destruction.

In Matthew 13:18–23, Jesus explains:

> 19 When anyone hears the word about the kingdom and doesn't understand it, the evil one comes and snatches away what was sown in his heart. This is the one sown along the path.
>
> Matthew 13:19 CSB

The enemy does not want the wisdom of God to be heard, understood, or followed. He wants us to be ignorant, deaf, mute, and blind so we can be led to destruction rather than saved in the arms of the Lord.

> [20] And the one sown on rocky ground—this is one who hears the word and immediately receives it with joy. [21] But he has no root and is short-lived. When distress or persecution comes because of the word, immediately he falls away.
>
> Matthew 13:20-21 CSB

This is the daughter who hears and values the Word but has no foundation or consistency. Without accountability or encouragement, she reverts to old ways.

> [22] Now the one sown among the thorns—this is one who hears the word, but the worries of this age and the deceitfulness of wealth choke the word, and it becomes unfruitful.
>
> Matthew 13:22 CSB

This is the daughter who hears the Word but is distracted by pleasing the world for money, status, and image. Her tree is bare.

> **23** But the one sown on the good ground—this is one who hears and understands the word, who does produce fruit and yields: some a hundred, some sixty, some thirty times what was sown.
>
> Matthew 13:23 CSB

This is the daughter who continues to be fruitful. Through consistent relationship with the Father: daily praying, fasting, giving, and serving, her tree bears fruit for those who are unable. She multiplies what she has received and feeds others who lack.

Her seed has the power to rebirth a generation of godly women committed to faith, sacrifice, and honor. Her teachings and wisdom will restore the broken, imprisoned, and fallen daughters of God. We must learn to be vulnerable and allow the Lord to father us, so we can walk fully in the blessings of His righteous daughters.

Prayer: For The Sower

Father,

I humble myself before You, the Creator of Life. Thank You for planting seeds of righteousness in Your daughter, even when her fruits and bearings were covered with soot and shame. Lord, You continue to keep her watered and filled with Your goodness through mercy and grace that she does not deserve. Forgive your daughter, Father, if she has planted harmful seeds in others: seeds born from hurt, jealousy, pride, or pain. Forgive her for wounding those who were longing for connection and whom she misled through her own brokenness. Help Your daughter plant new seeds in this world: seeds that bear the fruit of Your Spirit and continue to flourish, multiplying the works of Your Kingdom. May these seeds be a reflection of the place You have prepared for us in Your coming. Thank You for this moment in Your presence. I lift You up in all of my ways.

In Jesus' Name,

Amen

Chapter 9

Visit gemsrooted.org for resources

CHAPTER 10

Her Ministry

Your first ministry is God. Our Father has created us with such a unique purpose; in every detail of His plan, there are instructions we must listen to and obey. Ministry is a gift. It is the call to serve others and worship the Lord in all we do through submission and reverence.

As daughters, many of us desire marriage so we can be a wife to a man, grow a family, and be seen as desirable and favored. One must understand that this desire requires maturity, wisdom, and sacrifice. How can we demonstrate to God, the One who knows our thoughts and pure intentions, that we are ready for marriage? Is it because we simply want to be loved or live happily ever after? That may be our story, but it must begin with God's.

Marriage is a ministry, not a mindset. Unfortunately, society has taught us to defile the essence of marriage by adopting false doctrines and worldly covenants between man and status. There is a growing disconnect among young women today who believe status is the ultimate measure of happiness and longevity. In truth, marriage requires submission: first to God, then to her husband.

What is your ministry? How long have you been running from it, delaying it, or unclear about its progress?

If you are in constant connection with God, you will not miss the daily instructions or fine details of your ministry. You have been given a spiritual gift that no one else can duplicate. Serving the Lord with your God-given gifts by serving others is an act of pure worship.

The power of God flows through the delicate hands and obedient hearts of His. She is a garden who bears fruits of grace, wisdom, and beauty while basking under the love, care, and spiritual guidance of her Heavenly Father. Her assignment is to bring joy and love, not just through the presence of God, but by honoring Him through obedience and worship.

Some daughters are still waiting for the Lord to confirm their assignment. Others have already received the green light but continue to stumble over the details, falling into impatience, stagnation, distraction, or disobedience. But God, in His mercy, continues to send reminders of His love and encourages us through the Holy Spirit to move forward.

Yet sometimes, due to frustration or selfishness, we lose sight of our ministry and its purpose. Remember, your ministry aligns with your worship.

Our carnal desires can hinder our progress, leading to hostility and hopelessness. We must be vigilant when working in the ministry God has assigned to us and mindful of how our decisions impact our spiritual growth. Disobedience creates room for disdain, doubt, depression, and ultimately, spiritual death.

How can we lead, mentor, or teach others if we ourselves are walking in false hope or manipulation?

God wants to release the blessings our hearts long for, but first, we must be honest about where we truly stand in our ministry. Do not give doubt your time any longer. Stay focused on what the Lord has instructed you to do.

If you are unsure, ask Him to reveal it. He will, but you must be vulnerable enough to listen.

Sometimes, God places people in our path to realign us with His will. Speak to wise counsel; those with a genuine relationship with God. Lastly, do not rely on the opinions of others. Not all who claim to walk with God are privy to your personal conversations with the Father.

Prayer: For Her Ministry

Father,

I thank You for giving Your daughter gifts to spread Your love and power through the ministry You have called her to. Thank You for sending love notes to the world through daily encounters. At times, Your daughter may have put her wants before the needs of the ministry; however, Lord, give her direction as she navigates this season of obedience and vulnerability. Open her heart, mind, and eyes to seek first Your Kingdom. Help her be led by Your voice and presence in all that she does. I give it all to You, Father, in worship and in prayer.

In Jesus' Name,

Amen

Chapter 10

Visit gemsrooted.org for resources

CHAPTER 11

Her Chase

She follows after God's heart, love, and wisdom. She dances in humility, praising and exalting Him before the world. She sings of His victories and heals wounded hearts with His biblical love notes. His name remains steady on her lips as she pours out every detail, every minor thing, before her heavenly Father.

To be so greatly loved, even in her flaws and faltering moments, is to be held by the Lord who adores, protects, provides, and positions her in His divine timing. His love is unwavering. His sovereignty remains forever unshaken. His covenant from the womb, that includes the softness of His comfort and the firmness of His Word echo from ancient days.

Her first true experience of love came through the eyes of our Lord Jesus Christ. Her relationship stands on solid ground, rich with seeds ready to sprout spiritual fruit. She shares her testimony through life's challenges, defeating every battle with the Lord beside her. She praises through tested surrender, sacrifices what is temporary, and presses on in obedience.

Prayer

Father,

Thank You that the mundane and spiritual battles belong to You, not me. I pray that Your daughter will seek the guidance of Your Word and tear down the altars of this world. Let her rebuild them with righteous Arks: placed in the homes of Your people, where You, Lord, will dwell and be exalted as the "Lord of Armies."

In Jesus' Name,

Amen

Chapter 11
Visit gemsrooted.org for resources

CHAPTER 12

Her Willingness

The Lord provides grace, mercy, deliverance, and and protection daily. She seeks to attain her character from the Father and to surrender her ways unto the Lord. Better to live foolishly and feel the wrath of God than to live wisely and feel the wrath of this world. The hands of humans hold no mercy and are continually wrapped in deception. However, our Father, is just and merciful. He teaches through love, wisdom, patience, and favor.

Prayer:

Father,

If You will it so, let all Your daughter's ways reflect Your Spirit. Count the hairs on her head as a sacrifice: a living offering of faith and perseverance. Let her surrender to You forever. Let Your will be done in her. Teach her to be patient, slow to anger, and understanding toward her foes. Let the generosity of humility wash over her. Instill in her the knowledge of You, to be applied daily, that she may align my steps with the purposes of Your will. Let Your daughter no longer move in ignorance, but in pursuit of Your heart. Let her feast no more on the idle spoils of this world, but fill the pit of her belly with the fruits of the Spirit. May Your daughter forever reign in Your presence.

In Jesus' Name,

Amen

Chapter 12

Visit gemsrooted.org for resources

CHAPTER 13

To Be Human

²⁴ Jesus, however, would not entrust himself
to them, since he knew them all ²⁵ and because he did not need anyone to testify about
man; for he himself knew what was in man.

John 2:24-25 CSB

We were created in God's image: endowed with purpose, spiritual gifts, intellect, and the capacity for relationship. Jesus revealed Himself to the world without hesitation. On the contrary, we often hide behind masks and carefully curated personas, hoping for the world's approval and chasing temporary crowns.

Jesus modeled something greater: the art of letting go. He surrendered His earthly vessel in obedience, and in doing so, defeated death and was clothed in glory.

Each night we lay our heads down unaware of the fact that we are releasing battles from the day before. Each morning, fresh mercy is given to us, not just to survive, but to realign our thoughts and actions with Christ.

The cross He asks us to carry isn't just symbolic; it bears the weight of broken relationships, daily stress, emotional exhaustion, and spiritual inconsistency. It is the narrow road and it is costly. Jesus knew we would face these things. He knew it would be hard to surrender. He knew the ache of being human. Despite our challenges, He left us provision, wisdom, and tools to walk the road well.

As daughters, our surrender is also deeply intimate. We wrestle with vulnerability, trust, and letting God lead. We must remember that He is not a man that He should lie. He is our Father, and He fills every gap this world leaves empty (Numbers 23:19).

Prayer:

Father,

I bow before You today and ask: open Your daughter's heart to Your Word. Let her life be aligned with Your truth, and let it show in every action she commits and encounter she has. You made her in Your image. I repent on behalf of Your daughter for every distorted thought and every selfish pursuit. Restore her discipline and hunger for righteousness. Let Your holy will take root in her heart. Purify her appetite and remove her taste for sin. Let Your daughter crave after you. Make Your daughter pleasing in Your sight. Restore her zeal, and let her life retell the love story of Jesus Christ

In Jesus' Name,

Amen

Chapter 13

Visit gemsrooted.org for resources

CHAPTER 14

Stretching Her Beyond Her Comfort

The Father has birthed you with heavenly gifts: gifts you may have thought were once impossible to achieve.. Though those around you may look and wonder what keeps you going, it is the anointing that God has placed over your life. Your calling is a sacred bond between you and your Heavenly Father that He instilled in you from the womb. He knows exactly what your limits and capabilities are, and He sees the full potential of your achievements.

Do not allow the comforts of this world to disrupt your calling through compromise and deceit. God has no limits, and neither do His gifts and blessings for you. Age, mobility, finances, and knowledge hold no authority over your life. God, as the Creator of all things, has already planned every concern and detail about you. Trust in the Lord with all your heart's desires, for He knows the deepest places of your mind.

Place your burdens on Him, and allow Him to part the troubled waters of your history, relationships, and unforgiven memories that echo the lies of the enemy. God is with you always and will never forsake you. A father will carry his daughter to the ends of the earth before allowing anything to swallow her whole. Remember who you are. Do not let anyone accuse you when God has already cleansed you and made you whole. You are a Daughter of the King.

Prayer:

Father,

I come before You bringing the needs of my dear sister in Christ; she who continues to seek validation in the eyes of a blinded world. She is preparing to take on a new task that will shift the trajectory of her life and the lives of others. Lord, she needs You. She needs You to show up for her in ways she has not yet recognized as Your presence. With my hands over her crown, I pray: may she hear Your voice in her heart, fill her ears with the songs of Your truth, and move in step with the rhythm of Your Spirit in this season of feeling unfulfilled. Renew her mind, Lord. Help her to seek Your instructions, so that she may honor You in all her ways and worship You with her whole heart. Father, thank You for the opportunity You have given me to be an encourager, to speak life into the tender-hearted who seek Your love and understanding.

In Jesus' Name,

Amen

Chapter 14

Visit gemsrooted.org for resources

CHAPTER 15

You

I am a child of God. I am a daughter of the one true Savior, Jesus Christ. In His creation, God formed me and placed within me abilities, assignments, traits, and characteristics that reflect who He is.

In a world full of distractions, we often lose sight of who we truly are. We begin to identify ourselves by the world's standards: chasing its definitions, meeting its expectations, and forgetting we were created for something greater.

This is not our final mold. We are being continuously shaped by the precious hands of God. There is a crowning taking place: a spiritual birthing that calls for deliverance, deliberate obedience, and surrender. These qualities define who I truly am. I cannot be made of mud or failed ground. I must be shaped in the right hands: Christ's and not the world's.

The world is broken, and at times, so are we. We try to build ourselves without direction or the right tools. We let the world shape us. We fall into the enemy's trap, allowing him to chisel away the very parts God sees as beautiful. We are trained to focus on our flaws and feel unworthy. However, God created us with intention. We must learn to speak His truth, fall in love with His message, and trust the words He has written to guide and strengthen us.

Too often, we lose sight, faith, and identity. We chase empty words and search for meaning in all the wrong places. We try to define ourselves by the stars, symbols, and self-made ideas of purpose and power. They did not create themselves and they did not create us. Ignorantly, we give them names, power, and loyalty.

In doing so, we forget that we are not our own creators. We start saying, "I'll do things my way. His name doesn't fit me. I'll define myself." In that moment, we idolize ourselves. We become our gods, worshipping our plans, and wondering why we fall. We walk in pride. We boast.

We create our titles, our truths, our kingdoms...but they are not God's.

Prayer:

Father,

Thank you for opening your daughter's eyes to the deception of the world and the schemes of the enemy. Thank You for showing her that wisdom keeps her close to You. As daughters, help us to seek Your will, speak truth instead of falsehoods, and remember that our final mold is shaped by Your hands alone. Thank You for keeping us, teaching us, and preserving us in Your divine timing. I trust that our crowning is not of this world, but will take place in Your presence.

In Jesus' Name,
Amen

Chapter 15

Visit gemsrooted.org for resources

www.ingramcontent.com/pod-product-compliance
Lightning Source LLC
Chambersburg PA
CBHW061708120626
46550CB00003B/1148